Is it hot or cold?

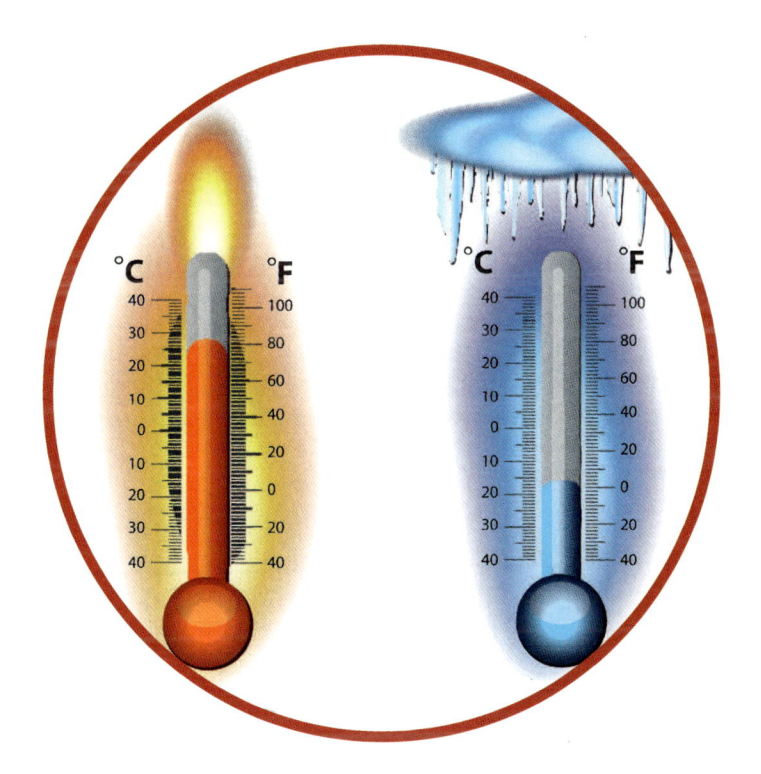

Susan Hughes

Crabtree Publishing Company
www.crabtreebooks.com

What's the Matter?

Author: Susan Hughes
Publishing plan research and development:
  Sean Charlebois, Reagan Miller
  Crabtree Publishing Company
Project development: Clarity Content Services
Project management: Karen Iversen
Project coordinator: Kathy Middleton
Editors: Susan Hughes, Kathy Middleton
Copy editor: Dimitra Chronopoulos
Proofreader: Reagan Miller
Design: First Image
Photo research: Linda Tanaka
Prepress technician: Katherine Berti
Print and production coordinator: Katherine Berti

Photographs:
p1 Monika Hunácková/shutterstock; p4 left iStockphoto/Thinkstock, Egal/dreamstime.com; p5 Monia/BIGSTOCK; p6 Rossario/shutterstock; p7 Rene Jansa/shutterstock; p8 Iofoto/shutterstock; p9 left Robert Wolkaniec/shutterstock, Kim Reinick/shutterstock; p10 iStockphoto/Thinkstock; p11 ppart/shutterstock; p13 top oliveromg/shutterstock, Maszas/dreamstime.com; p14 Hemera/Thinkstock; p15 top Cogipix/dreamstime.com, dragon_fang/shutterstock; p16 ChameleonsEye/shutterstock; p17 Alhovik/shutterstock; p18 Andrey Eremin/shutterstock; p19 top JanPietruszka/BIGSTOCK, Sparkia/BIGSTOCK; p20 Masr/dreamstime.com; p21 Battrick/shutterstock; p22 Gaby Kooijman/shutterstock; cover shutterstock

---

Library and Archives Canada Cataloguing in Publication

Hughes, Susan, 1960-
    Is it hot or cold? / Susan Hughes.

(What's the matter?)
Includes index.
Issued also in electronic formats.
ISBN 978-0-7787-2049-2 (bound).--ISBN 978-0-7787-2056-0 (pbk.)

    1. Heat--Juvenile literature. 2. Cold--Juvenile literature. 3. Temperature--Juvenile literature. 4. Matter--Properties--Juvenile literature. I. Title. II. Series: What's the matter? (St. Catharines, Ont.)

QC256.H84 2012   j620.1'1296   C2012-900293-3

Library of Congress Cataloging-in-Publication Data

Hughes, Susan, 1960-
Is it hot or cold? / Susan Hughes.
p. cm. -- (What's the matter?)
Includes index.
ISBN 978-0-7787-2049-2 (reinforced library binding : alk. paper) --
ISBN 978-0-7787-2056-0 (pbk. : alk. paper) -- ISBN 978-1-4271-7947-0 (electronic pdf) -- ISBN 978-1-4271-8062-9 (electronic html)
 1. Temperature--Juvenile literature. 2. Matter--Properties--Juvenile literature.
I. Title.

QC271.4.H84 2012
536--dc23
                                        2012000120

Crabtree Publishing Company

www.crabtreebooks.com   1-800-387-7650

Printed in the U.S.A./032012/CJ20120215

Copyright © **2012 CRABTREE PUBLISHING COMPANY**. All rights reserved. No part of this publication may be reproduced, stored in a retrieval system or be transmitted in any form or by any means, electronic, mechanical, photocopying, recording, or otherwise, without the prior written permission of Crabtree Publishing Company. In Canada: We acknowledge the financial support of the Government of Canada through the Canada Book Fund for our publishing activities.

Published in Canada
Crabtree Publishing
616 Welland Ave.
St. Catharines, ON
L2M 5V6

Published in the United States
Crabtree Publishing
PMB 59051
350 Fifth Avenue, 59th Floor
New York, New York 10118

Published in the United Kingdom
Crabtree Publishing
Maritime House
Basin Road North, Hove
BN41 1WR

Published in Australia
Crabtree Publishing
3 Charles Street
Coburg North
VIC 3058

What is in this book?

What is matter? 4
What are properties? 6
Is it hot? 8
Is it cold? 10
What is temperature? 12
Temperature clues 14
Using a thermometer 16
Melting 18
Freezing 20
Hot and cold! 22
Words to know and Index 23
Notes for adults 24

What is matter?

How are a cold popsicle and a mug of hot chocolate the same?

They are both made of **matter**. Everything is made of matter.

You are made of matter, too! Matter is anything that takes up space and has **mass**.

Mass is the amount of material in an object.

What are properties?

Matter has **properties**.

Properties describe how something looks, feels, tastes, smells, or sounds.

We can look at something to see if it is big or small.

We can feel if something is **hot** or **cold**.

Size and temperature are properties.

Is it hot?

Different materials have different properties.

Some materials are hot.

The oven is hot. It cooks our food.

The kettle makes water hot for coffee or tea.

The toaster makes the bread hot.

Why do all of these objects need to be hot?

Is it cold?

Some materials are cold.

The ice pack is cold.

It helps get rid of headaches.

The refrigerator is cold.

It keeps food fresh.

Think about something you ate today. Was it hot or cold?

What is temperature?

Temperature is a kind of measurement.

It tells us how hot or cold something is.

A low temperature means something is cold.

A high temperature means something is hot.

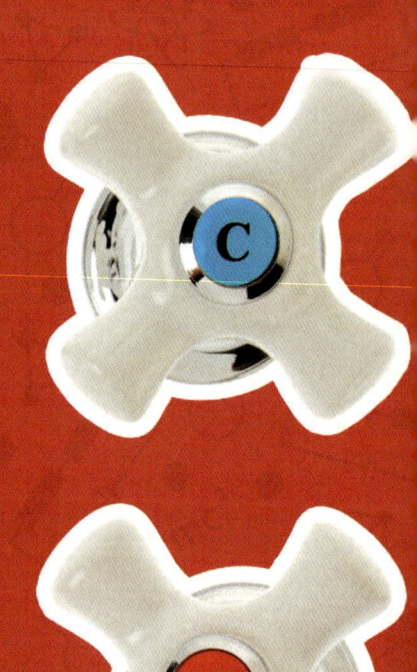

It is usually cold in winter.

The temperature can be very low.

It is usually hot in summer.

The temperature can be very high.

? How can looking outside help you to decide what to wear?

Temperature clues

We use clues to figure out the temperature outside.

We know it is cold outside if we see snow on the ground.

What other clues tell us about the temperature outside?

We use clues to figure out the temperature of objects, too.

Are these peas hot or cold?

Is the butter in this pan hot or cold?

How do you know?

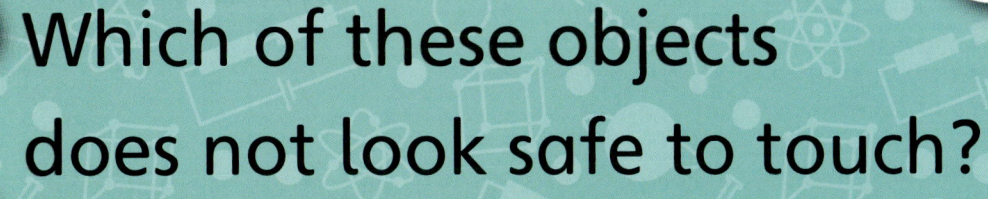

Which of these objects does not look safe to touch?

Using a thermometer

Is it so cold outside that you will need to wear a coat?

To find out, you can look at a **thermometer**.

A thermometer is a tool that measures the temperature of the air outside.

The numbers on a thermometer are called **degrees**. Degrees show how much heat is in the air.

Most thermometers have a glass tube with **liquid** inside.

The liquid moves up to a higher number when it is hot outside.

The liquid moves down to a lower number when it gets cold.

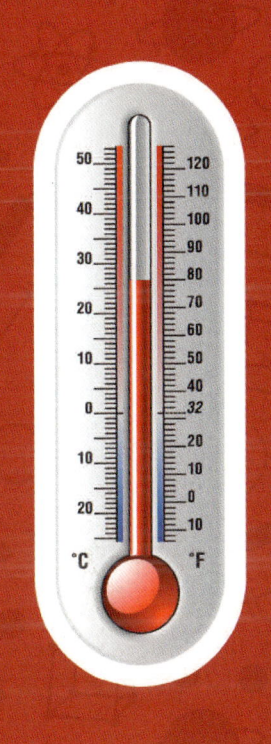

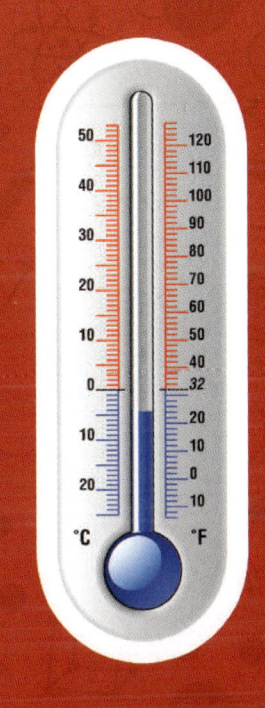

Melting

Some objects change when their temperature changes.

An ice cube is frozen water.

Take an ice cube out of the freezer.

The temperature inside the freezer was very low. The temperature outside of the freezer is higher.

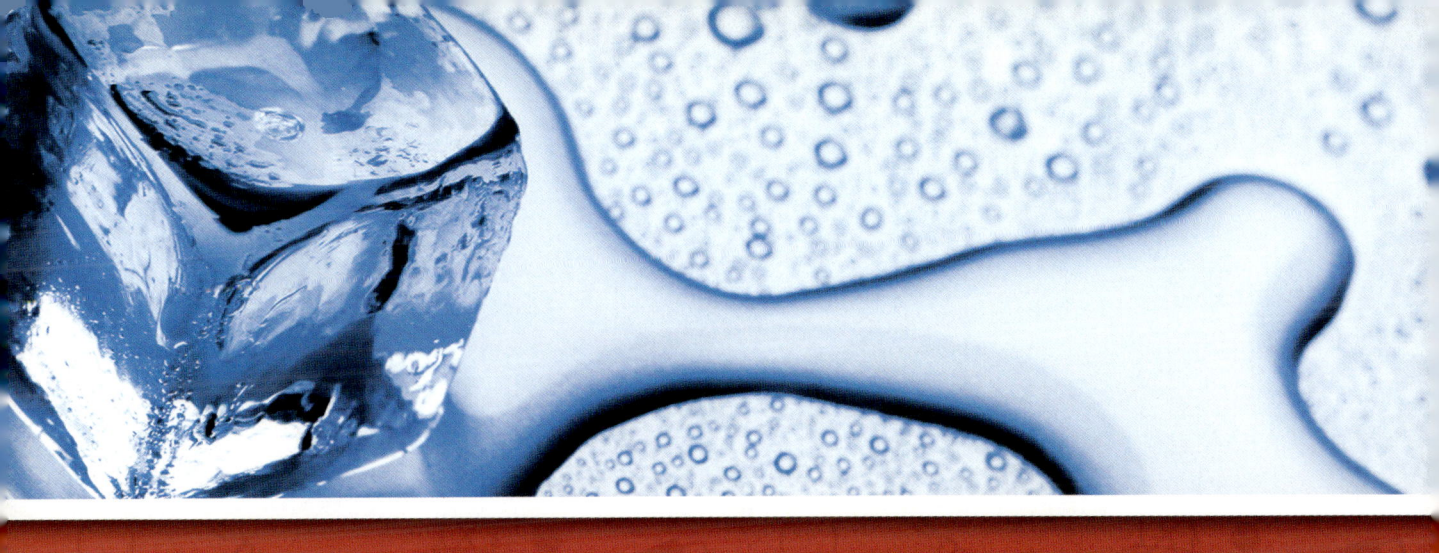

The ice cube begins to **melt** in the warmer temperature.

It turns back into water.

What happens when you take too long to eat an ice-cream cone?

Freezing

What happens when you put water in the freezer?

It **freezes**.
It turns to ice.

Water freezes when the temperature is at the **freezing point**, or below.

The freezing point of water is 32 degrees Fahrenheit or 0 degrees Celsius.

This thermometer shows the temperature at the freezing point.

Does your family have a thermometer at home? Is it inside or outside?

Hot and cold!

A lunch bag and a thermos can keep food hot or cold.

You can choose!

What hot and cold things would you like to pack for your lunch today?

Words to know and Index

cold
pages 4, 7, 10–11, 12–13, 14–15, 16–17, 22

hot
pages 4, 7, 8–9, 11, 12–13, 15, 17, 22

mass
page 5

matter
pages 4–5, 6

properties
pages 6–7, 8

temperature
pages 7, 12–13, 14–15, 16, 18, 20, 21

thermometer
pages 16–17, 21

Notes for adults

Objectives
- to introduce children to hot and cold and to the processes of melting and freezing
- to learn how people can measure temperature

Prerequisite
Ask the children to read *Is it flexible or rigid?* before reading *Is it hot or cold?* Introducing them to the concepts of matter via *Is it flexible or rigid?* will help familiarize them with the initial concepts in this book.

Questions before reading *Is it hot or cold?*
"What things are hot? What things are cold?"

"What are your favorite foods? Are they hot or cold?"

"What do you wear outside on a hot day?"

"How is what you wear on a hot day different than what you wear on a cold day?"

Discussion
Read the book to the children. Discuss with them some of the main concepts in the book, such as hot and cold, temperature, and thermometer.

Show the children a thermometer and point out the freezing point of water (32 degrees Fahrenheit and 0 degrees Celsius). Have children point to a place on the thermometer that shows it is a hot day, and a place that shows it is a cold day.

If you have access to a freezer, repeat the steps to melt ice cubes and freeze water (pages 18–21).

Extension
Create a list on the board with two columns: Hot foods and Cold foods. Have the children offer suggestions for each column. Discuss how we keep food cold and why, and how we make food hot and why.